Process Theology and Biblical Interpretation

Topical Line Drives, Volume 45

Ronald L. Farmer

Energion Publications
Gonzalez, Florida
2021

ISBN: 978-1-63199-746-4
eISBN: 978-1-63199-747-1

Energion Publications
P. O. Box 841
Gonzalez, Florida 32560

energion.com
pubs@energion.com

Dedication
To Patricia,
My partner in the adventure of life

TABLE OF CONTENTS

1   How Am I to Read the Bible?
    The Quest for a Satisfying Hermeneutic   1

2   The Importance of "Glasses":
    The Power of Presuppositions   5

3   Building a "Toolbox":
    The "Tools" of Biblical Interpretation   12

4   Key Components of a Process Approach
    to Biblical Interpretation   19

5   An Application of a Process Hermeneutic:
    Revelation 4-5   25

    Suggested Readings on Process Hermeneutics   38

CHAPTER ONE

How Am I to Read the Bible?
The Quest for a Satisfying Hermeneutic

Introduction

My first exposure to the theological and ethical use of the Bible was in the context of the fundamentalist Protestant church of my childhood. Almost weekly, I listened to "biblically-based" sermons espousing patriarchy and sexism, racism and speciesism, paternalism and unfettered capitalism, imperialism and militarism. Such teachings clashed with the youthful personal convictions I was formulating based on my own experience and educational journey, especially my high school natural and social sciences courses. Because the pastor stressed how important it is to "accurately divide the word of truth" (he loved to quote 2 Tim 2:15—from the King James Version, of course), I came to view the Bible and the church as agents of oppression. As is frequently the case when people are forced to choose between intellect and religion—a crisis all too common when the only form of religion known is fundamentalist in nature—I left the church.

Toward the end of my undergraduate college years, an existential crisis reawakened deep spiritual concerns that had lain dormant for almost five years. Fortunately, my former church had recently called a pastor who held more moderate theological convictions and was interested in reaching out intellectually to college students. I found his sermons to be generally compatible with my educational and life experiences—which confused me. You see, like the previous fundamentalist pastor, the new pastor also claimed that his sermons were "biblically based." How could two pastors read the same Bible yet preach radically different sermons? Which pastor was "accurately dividing the word of truth?" Did the Bible promote oppression or liberation? Or to phrase my confusion succinctly, "How was I to read the Bible?"

1

I began to meet with the new pastor weekly in an effort to answer this question. Although I did not know the terminology at that time, I had embarked on a quest for a satisfying hermeneutic.[1] Little did I know that this quest would lead me to seminary, on to graduate school, and finally to a career as a professor of New Testament and an ordained minister of a progressive Christian denomination.

From the Beginning of the Quest to the Impasse[2]

Not surprisingly, my quest for a satisfying hermeneutic in many respects paralleled the history of modern biblical interpretation. Like a starving man moving along a cafeteria line, I "spooned out" generous helpings of all the offerings: one after another I immersed myself in the historical-critical method, classical liberalism's progressive revelation, the Biblical Theology Movement, Bultmann's existentialist interpretation, the New Hermeneutic, liberation criticism, feminist criticism, literary criticism, and finally deconstructionism. Imagine my disappointment when, after years of exploration and experimentation, my quest for a satisfying hermeneutic brought me to an impasse. Never mind that the same impasse had been encountered by many others who reflected deeply on the current state of the hermeneutical enterprise. Shared disappointment is disappointment still. Let me elaborate.

Although there were elements of each hermeneutical method that seemed useful, even essential, for the theological and ethical appropriation of the Bible, I did not find any one method that I could embrace completely. Consequently, I found myself engaged in what I refer to as "toolbox raiding," that is, using a "tool" from one methodology in combination with a "tool" from an entirely different methodology. Understandably, methodological purists

---

1 The word "hermeneutics" is a noun derived from the Greek verb *hermeneuō*, "to interpret, to explain." For a concise definition of hermeneutics, "a theory and methodology of interpretation" will suffice for now. I will delve deeper into this word and several related terms in a future chapter.

2 For a detailed account of this phase of my quest, see Ronald L. Farmer, *Beyond the Impasse: The Promise of a Process Hermeneutic*, Studies in American Biblical Hermeneutics 13 (Macon, GA: Mercer UP, 1997) 3-46.

frowned upon my eclecticism, but that did not concern me. Methodological purists, you see, engage in a limitation of meaning; that is, they create meaning acceptable to *self-enclosed communities* who share the same methodological approach. I, however, was interested in reopening *public discourse* on the Bible, so the criticism of methodological purists did not concern me. No, what troubled me, what deeply disturbed me, was that "my use of these divergent tools was entirely *ad hoc.* [3] The various hermeneutical approaches from which I borrowed were based on diverse, even conflicting, perspectives and presuppositions; I had no undergirding methodological rationalization for my eclecticism."[4]

Even worse, several of the newer hermeneutical methodologies called into question the idea that language actually refers to something external to the user. Earlier Bultmann and others had called into question the idea of speaking *meaningfully and truthfully about God-in-Godself* with the in/famous assertion that "all theology is anthropology." Instead of speaking meaningfully about God, we are actually talking about ourselves. More recently, deconstructionism moved beyond Bultmann by calling into question the very notion of *referentiality in language.* Can one speak meaningfully of and to the "real external world," or are we *locked in a linguistic universe where words only refer to other words*? Instead of speaking meaningfully and truthfully about the real external world, *are we merely playing language games* that are only meaningful to those who follow the same rules for the language game? Clearly my quest had reached an impasse.

BEYOND THE IMPASSE

A few years after graduate school, my wife[5] introduced me to the process philosophy of Alfred North Whitehead. Although

---

3 The Latin phrase *ad hoc* (lit. "to this") signifies a solution designed for a specific situation; it is not generalizable or intended to be applied to other situations.

4 Farmer, *Beyond the Impasse* 46.

5 My wife, Patricia Adams Farmer, wrote the volume in the Topical Line Drive Series entitled *Beauty and Process Theology: A Journey of Transformation* (Energion 2020). She is also the author of two collections of process-inspired essays, *Embracing a Beautiful* God (Chalice 2003;

my initial investigations were confined to theological and philo-sophical matters (for example, God and the problem of evil), I soon discovered that process thought had exciting implications for the development of a hermeneutic. I threw myself into a study of Whitehead focusing on his understanding of perception and language in the attempt to develop a process method for reading texts. My hope, my intuition, was that the development of a process hermeneutic would lead me beyond the impasse.

Before describing the key components of a process hermeneu-tic and examining how a process-informed theory of interpretation can greatly advance our theological and ethical appropriation of the Bible, I must first discuss the vitally important—albeit often overlooked—role presuppositions play.

anniversary ed. Estrella de Mar 2013) and *Fat Soul: A Philosophy of S-I-Z-E* (Shiprock 2016); co-editor (with Jay McDaniel) of *Replanting Ourselves in Beauty: Toward an Ecological Civilization* (Process Century 2015); and two philosophical novels, *The Metaphor Maker* (Estrella de Mar 2009) and its sequel, *The Fat Soul Society* (Estrella de Mar 2013).

Chapter Two

The Importance of "Glasses": The Power of Presuppositions

"Glasses" on the Micro Scale: Assumptions or Presuppositions

The goal of every honest biblical interpreter is to assist in making a text's meaning understandable to a contemporary reader. The technical term for this interpretive process is *exegesis*, a term derived from the Greek verb *exogeomai*, "to lead out." Applied to texts, *exegesis* refers to the "leading or reading out" of meaning. The goal is to bring meaning *out of* the biblical text. The interpreter is to avoid *eisegesis*, the reading of meaning *into* the text. Although gross *eisegesis* should be avoided, one must acknowledge that a reader does not "emerge" from a text with a meaning gathered exclusively from within, like pulling something out of a bag. The reader must first get *into* the text by means of asking questions of the text, and some of those questions likely were not in the mind of the author. Thus, to some degree, *eisegesis* is inevitable.

No one approaches the reading of the Bible as a totally objective "blank slate." On the contrary, all interpreters approach the Bible with certain "presuppositions" or "assumptions" in place that largely determine the meaning they are able to "see" when they read the text. These presuppositions can be consciously embraced, although most often they are unconsciously held, having been absorbed—as if by social "osmosis"—from the dominate culture.

Another way we can describe the situation of the interpreter is to say that everyone views the world from a particular historical, cultural, and linguistic "perspective" or "standpoint," and to acknowledge that this perspective is always partial, never comprehensive or absolute or complete. Metaphorically speaking, we can say that all interpreters wear "glasses." Now as anyone who wears physical glasses will tell you, you can actually forget that you are wearing physical glasses; likewise, we can forget that we are wearing these metaphorical glasses. In fact, many people are not even aware that they *are* wearing these "glasses"; and because they are not aware, they assume that everyone sees the world in the same manner as they do. So in addition to clarifying that everyone wears these metaphorical glasses, we must also acknowledge that no one wears glasses with clear lenses, although it is common for people to think they do. For example, how often has someone with whom you disagree on some topic asked you, "Can't you see? It's as plain as the nose on your face."

The truth is, every interpreter reads the biblical text looking through "tinted lenses." Moreover, no two interpreters wear glasses with exactly the same tint in the lenses because the tint is the result of the experiences each interpreter has had. To the degree that two interpreters have had similar life experiences, they will have a similar tint to their glasses; to the degree they have had different life experiences, their respective tints will differ. Because different interpreters wear glasses with lenses in a variety of tints, they will inevitably "see" different things when they read a text—or when they "look" at anything else, for that matter.

Given the fact that everyone wears metaphorical glasses, what are honest interpreters to do if they are to achieve their goal of making a text's meaning understandable to a contemporary reader? First, they should try to describe (as best they can) the "tint of their own glasses." This self-conscious activity can be quite enlightening! Second, when they hear or read the interpretations of others, they should seek to describe the "tint in the other interpreters' glasses" that logically led them to their interpretations of the text. By seeking to understand your own perspective (presuppositions), and the perspectives (presuppositions) of others, you will avoid the mistaken notion that you (or they) have arrived at THE totally objective/absolute truth. Instead, you will realize that truth, as far as *finite* humans can discover it, is always *partial* and *perspectival*. (To claim that a human can attain absolute truth would be to claim that a finite human being is capable of seeing from all perspectives— that is, to claim that one is divine!) Thus, your reading of the text may indeed be *truthful*, it might even be *better* than other proposed readings, but it cannot be THE truth because you cannot escape the perspectival nature of your reading.

An important component in describing the "tint" in these metaphorical glasses—one's own as well as others—is to be aware of how presuppositions/assumptions work on a cultural scale.

"Glasses" on the Macro Scale: Worldviews

Thus far, I have described how our "presuppositional lenses" determine what we see, how we think, what arguments we find convincing, and so forth. On a larger scale, these lenses are manifestations of the "worldview" we have adopted. As with their general assumptions, most people have *unconsciously* adopted the worldview of the dominant culture in which they live. Others, however, have been more *self-conscious* about the process. The primary goal of this chapter is to assist readers in becoming self-conscious about their metaphorical glasses. A basic knowledge of the four worldviews that have dominated the West are crucial for this undertaking.[6]

(1) **Cosmic Empathy**—Cosmic empathy is the earliest of these worldviews that scholars have been able to identify. The ancient world was understood to be thoroughly interrelated. Humans, animals, plants, and rocks all participated in the same cosmic, life-giving power. This belief is often referred to as "animism." Later, belief in multiple gods and goddesses arose as personifications of what we today would refer to as natural phenomena.

(2) **The Dominant Medieval Worldview**—The next dominant worldview arose from two influences: Hebrew monotheism and Greek philosophy. The notion of one God who created all things and acts in the history of the Hebrew people resulted in several significant developments: (a) a shift from viewing the cycles of nature as the primary religious focus, to a linear view of history and a future hope as the religious focus; (b) a heightened moral consciousness because God was understood to be moral; (c) a movement away from the belief of male and female deities, to belief

---

6 For another overview of Western worldviews as it relates to the interpretation of the Bible, see: Russell Pregeant, *Encounter with the New Testament: An Interdisciplinary Approach* (Fortress, 2009) 24-28.

in one God who was primarily, although not exclusively, referred to as male; (d) understanding God as transcendent to nature resulted in a gradual desacralization or demystication of nature. (For the Hebrews, God was sovereign over nature; humans were to be stewards of nature for God. The reader should take account of the dramatic change that occurs during the modern period.)

Greek philosophy was the second influence that contributed to the rise of the second dominant worldview in the West. The shift away from worshiping nature deities to worshiping the deities of Mt. Olympus meant a shift away from focusing on nature to focusing on human civilization and political order. In keeping with Platonic thought, the "ideas" found in human civilization and political order were viewed as more real (and hence more representative of the divine realm) than was true of nature; thus, nature became viewed as "less real."

For more than a millennium, the marriage of Hebrew monotheism and Greek philosophy provided the dominant worldview of the West. A transcendent, all powerful God reigned over a physical universe arranged in a "great chain of being"—God and other "purely spiritual" beings at the top; then humans (who were thought of as composed of "matter" and "spirit"); and finally nature (which was thought of as composed only of "matter") at the bottom. As nature became more thoroughly desacralized over the centuries, it became a mere "object" for scientific study and a resource for economic exploitation; nature was thought to have no *inherent* value, only *instrumental* value.[7]

(3) **The Modern Worldview**—The modern period began with these long-held assumptions from the Medieval Worldview: supernaturalistic theism (an all-powerful God exists) and dualism (everything in the world is composed of little bits of matter in motion, with the exception of the human mind or soul, which is composed of spirit, like God). Over the next 300 years, however, theism collapsed into atheism (no God), and dualism collapsed into materialism (everything, including the so-called human mind, is composed of little bits of matter in motion). By the 20th Century,

---

7 One should also note that viewing reality as "a great chain of being" leads quite naturally to notions of hierarchy and empire—and all the ethical problems arising from those notions.

the resulting mechanistic determinism led many to despair, giving rise to existentialism (a last-ditch attempt to salvage "human freedom" and at least "subjective" meaning) and nihilism (the loss of all "objective" meaning). The world became conceived of as one colossal machine operating according to fixed mechanical, deterministic laws (that science could discover), and humans were merely insignificant cogs in this machine.

The following three problems contributed to this collapse of "supernaturalistic theism and dualism" to "atheistic materialism." (a) In *early* Modernism, God was needed to fill the "gaps" of scientific knowledge; but as the gaps became smaller and fewer in number, it made more sense in *later* Modernism to abandon the notion of God and simply allow science more time to find the answers. (b) The notion of an all-powerful God gives rise to the notoriously insoluble Problem of Evil. (c) The more the human "mind" or "soul" became associated with the physical brain, the more material and less spiritual it became; the "mind" came to be understood as simply a chain of neuro-chemical-electrical reactions in the physical brain.

Many people still held religious beliefs, of course, but it became increasingly difficult to offer convincing intellectual arguments within the framework of Modernity. For example, in the 20th Century, liberal Christians developed a form of theistic existentialism, while conservative Christians reverted to certain aspects of the pre-modern world (i.e., they rejected most modern science and embraced many ideas from the Medieval Worldview). To non-believers subscribing to the Modern Worldview, liberal Christianity sounds vacuous, and conservative Christianity is anti-intellectual.

(4) **The Postmodern Worldview**—The 20th Century also saw the emergence of a new way of thinking: "postmodernism." Many today see this as an emerging worldview. There are actually two forms: *deconstructive postmodernism*, which takes modernism to its logical conclusions (one philosopher calls it "most-modernism"[8]); and *constructive postmodernism*. Both forms are doubtful that humans can achieve *absolute* knowledge because human perception is always perspectival and partial. Deconstruction concludes

8 David Ray Griffin, *God & Religion in the Postmodern World* (SUNY, 1989) x, 8, 20.

from this that all claims to knowledge, truth, meaning, and religious belief are ultimately meaningless (except to the individual making the claims and others playing the same "language game"). According to the *deconstructive* postmodern worldview, all we have is a linguistic universe; all we have are word games, so God-talk is a word game we can play, but we should not think that the words correspond to anything in *reality*.

Constructive postmodernism draws a very different conclusion. Although human knowledge is limited by perspective, one can construct a *provisional* description of reality that is open to revision as new data are encountered. And without reverting to pre-modern ways of thinking, this *constructive* version of postmodernism emphasizes the interrelatedness of all things, thus leading to a respiritualizing and resacralizing of nature. God is no longer thought of as all-controlling and detached from the world; on the contrary, God is understood to be very much a part of the interrelatedness of reality. One could describe this understanding of God as "naturalistic theism" (in sharp contrast with the earlier supernaturalistic theism).

Simultaneous with the emergence of postmodern thought in philosophy, science was experiencing a radical change. Newtonian-based physics gave way to relativity, quantum physics, particle physics, field theory, string theory, and other versions of contemporary physics. Scientists discovered "indeterminacy" at the sub-atomic level of reality (corresponding to "freedom" at the human level); thus, the world is not a deterministic, mechanistic machine. Although it is hard to describe reality in terms of contemporary physics, clearly the expression "little bits of matter in motion" no longer fits. Something like "energy events" works better, a concept much more conducive to spirituality. Indeed, many of the leading physicists are quite interested in matters traditionally thought of as "spiritual questions."

"GLASSES": THE CURRENT STATUS

Now that we have discussed the power of assumptions or presuppositions and have surveyed the four worldviews that have dominated the West, an obvious question arises: What is the

10

current status with regard to Christianity in general and biblical interpretation in particular? Today, Christianity is quite divided—not so much along denominational lines but into "fundamentalist/conservative" Christians and "liberal/progressive" Christians. Both types of Christians are found in all denominations, although some denominations are predominantly conservative, and others are predominantly progressive. Conservative Christians tend to subscribe to a *mixture* of the Medieval Worldview and the Modern Worldview (e.g., they reject most of the *scientific* aspects of the Modern Worldview and replace them with aspects of the Medieval Worldview). Progressive Christians subscribe to the *constructive* version of the Postmodern Worldview. Thus, there is a sharp divide today—a divide that is apparent in the different ways Christians approach and interpret the Bible.

Process theology is one of the prime examples of progressive Christianity. A description of a process-informed approach to biblical interpretation will be undertaken in Chapter Four, but first, we must examine the notion of a metaphorical "toolbox" to accompany our metaphorical "glasses."

CHAPTER THREE

BUILDING A "TOOLBOX":
THE "TOOLS" OF BIBLICAL INTERPRETATION

INTRODUCTION

Just as a carpenter has a toolbox filled with tools to assist in performing a variety of tasks, so too the interpreter of the Bible has a toolbox filled with tools to assist in the interpretive process. And just as a carpenter's toolbox has trays to organize the various tools, so too the biblical interpreter's toolbox has "trays" that organize these tools. One tray holds literary tools; another tray, historical tools. A screwdriver, a hammer, and a saw enable a carpenter to accomplish different woodworking tasks; likewise, the various historical and literary tools enable the interpreter to discern different facets of a text's meaning. No one tool can exhaust a text's meaning; the interpreter must learn to use numerous tools in a complementary manner.

Each tool or method or approach to interpreting a text is called a "criticism." This is a technical expression used by scholars to denote a field of study that has developed defined principles and techniques. The English word "criticism" is derived from the Greek verb *krinein*, "to judge, to discern." Thus, the expression "biblical criticism" does not indicate that one is critical in the negative sense of being disparaging or contemptuous of the Bible; rather, biblical criticism refers to using one's critical faculties to guide the interpretive process. The goal of biblical exegesis, then, is to present "a coherent, informed interpretation" of a text "based on one's encounter with and investigation of a text at a given point in time."⁹ One's interpretation of a given text can change over time as (1) one has new experiences (e.g., as the tint in one's "glasses" alters), (2)

---

9 John H. Hayes and Carl R. Holladay, *Biblical Exegesis: A Beginners Handbook*, rev. ed. (Westminster John Knox, 1983, 1987, 2007) 23.

one develops greater knowledge in general and greater facility in the use of critical methodologies in particular, and (3) one grows spiritually. Thus, every exegesis should be presented with humility and an openness to listen to other proposed interpretations.

The purpose of this chapter is to survey the most important of these exegetical tools. Describing how and when to use the various tools is beyond the scope of this small volume. Numerous books provide such instruction,[10] and I plan to write a sequel to this book that will include such instruction and illustration. For now, however, let us simply open the "toolbox" and look through the "tools."

HISTORICAL TOOLS

The Bible is an historical document. It was written (and interpreted) in distinct historical and cultural settings and, of course, it refers to historical people, places, and events. Not surprisingly, biblical exegetes have developed tools to help them uncover the historical world of the Bible. Historical criticism approaches a biblical text as a "window" through which the interpreter seeks to view the past. The goal is to understand, to the degree it is possible, who wrote the text, when it was written, where it was written, who the original audience was, why the text was written, how the original audience interpreted the text, and similar historical questions.

All interpretations of the Bible need to undergo a test for validation. For historical criticism, the question to be asked is, "How well does the proposed historical reconstruction 'fit' all the available historical evidence?" Interpreters sometimes propose historical readings of a text that the available evidence does not support when other exegetes test the proposed interpretation. A proposed his-

---

10 In addition to Hayes and Holladay (see preceding footnote), an excellent place to begin is with freshman-level introductions to the Hebrew Bible/ Old Testament and New Testament, such as Christian E. Hauer and William A. Young, *An Introduction to the Bible: A Journey into Three Worlds* 8th ed. (Pearson, 2011); John J. Collins, *A Short Introduction to the Hebrew Bible*, 2nd ed. (Fortress, 2014); and Russell Pregeant, *Encounter with the New Testament: An Interdisciplinary Approach* (Fortress 2009). Also excellent are the volumes in the Society of Biblical Literature's *Guides to Biblical Scholarship* series (for example, *What Is Redaction Criticism?*), most of which are now published by Wipf and Stock.

torical interpretation will fall into one of four levels of certainty: impossible, improbable, possible, or probable. Because historical reconstruction occurs in the public arena, a proposed reading is always subject to correction and improvement as more evidence becomes available.

There are three types of historical study: (1) literary history, that is, a study of the historical development *of the text itself*; (2) empirical historical reconstruction of the history of the biblical period, that is, the history *in the text*; and (3) the history of the interpretation of the Bible by various Jewish and Christian communities, that is, the history of *the Bible's use*. To achieve the purpose of this volume, a discussion of the first two forms of historical study will suffice.

Tools for Reconstructing the History *of* the Biblical Text Itself

Most, though not all, of the biblical documents passed through the following stages in the course of their literary history: (a) an oral stage, when the biblical materials circulated by word of mouth; (b) eventually these oral traditions were written down, forming written sources; (c) these written sources were later combined and edited to form the biblical documents we possess; (d) these documents were copied by hand for centuries, which resulted in variant readings among the manuscripts we possess; and (e) at different points in time, the various biblical writings came to be accepted as scripture for the various Jewish and Christian communities.

(a) Tools for reconstructing the oral stage

Traditions criticism—This approach attempts to reconstruct the development of individual units of tradition within existing written texts in order to discover their origin and to trace how they were adapted as they were transmitted over time. As this description suggests, traditions criticism, although helpful, is speculative in nature.

Form criticism—This approach attempts to identify the literary genre (form) of individual units of tradition, with the goal of determining the "situation in life" in which these genres developed, especially during the oral period. The assumption is that certain social settings gave rise to certain literary forms. Like traditions criticism, form criticism is speculative in nature.

(b) Tool for reconstructing the written sources stage

Source criticism—This approach attempts to identify (if they still exist) or reconstruct (if they are not extant) the various written sources that were used in writing the various books of the Bible.

(c) Tool for reconstructing the editing of oral traditions, written sources, and earlier versions of biblical books into their final written versions

Redaction criticism—To "redact" is to edit preexisting material. This approach attempts to understand how and why the various oral traditions and written sources have been combined in the final written version of a biblical book. The goal is to discover the theological perspective of the final author/editor.

(d) Tool for reconstructing the transmission of the biblical books

Textual criticism—This approach attempts to reconstruct the original written text (the "autograph") by studying and comparing the various manuscripts known today. The significance of the invention of the printing press in 1450 cannot be overestimated. Handwritten copies were expensive and time-consuming; moreover, copying a lengthy document by hand always leads to errors, with no two copies exactly alike. The printing press standardized the text of the Bible.

(e) Tool for the reconstruction of the canonization process

Canonical criticism—This approach studies the biblical books in terms of their place in the collection recognized as authoritative in the various Jewish and Christian communities. Canonical criticism considers the whole to be more than the sum of its parts; moreover, the parts are to be read in light of the whole. A word of caution is in order: Because the believing community has already accepted the faith presented by (or *presumed* to be expressed in) the text, for the community there exists a "pre-understanding" of the text. Consequently, there is a tendency to ignore any differences, inconsistencies, and problems in the text.

Tools for Reconstructing the History *in* the Biblical Text

The goal of empirical historical research is to answer the question, What actually happened? Empirical reconstruction of the history *in* the Bible relies upon available, observable, and verifiable evidence, such as historical documents and archaeological data. Reconstructing the history *in* the Bible requires interpreters to use all the social scientific tools developed by such disciplines as history, archaeology, anthropology, sociology, and social psychology.

LITERARY TOOLS

The assumption underlying the literary study of the Bible is that biblical texts, like all texts, create *unique worlds of meaning* through their unique use of language. The goal of literary criticism is to understand the meaning of the text itself, *apart from anything outside it.* (Questions regarding references in the text to the external world of historical people and events are set aside.) The various forms of literary criticism described below seek to recreate, through careful description, the dynamics of this literary world created by the text. This description includes not only a text's *meaning* but also *how* it creates meaning. The criterion for judging the results of a literary critical reading is the text itself: Is the proposed reading faithful to the text?

Because each interpreter reads a text from a particular point of view ("glasses")—i.e., with particular presuppositions, at a particular point in history, and in a particular cultural setting—and because the biblical texts are rich, multifaceted, and polyvalent (as is the case with all good literature), numerous readings of a text are possible. Although some readings may be better or more insightful than others, there is no one correct literary interpretation.

Just as biblical interpreters engaging in historical criticism are able to resort to the academic disciples of the social sciences for well-honed tools to reconstruct the *history in the texts of the Bible*, so too biblical interpreters engaging in literary criticism are able to draw upon the academic discipline of literary analysis for well-tested tools for exploring the *unique literary worlds created by biblical texts*. The literary-critical approach to the Bible has been described as a breath of fresh air blowing through the dry and dusty corridors of the museum created by some forms of historical criticism. Whereas historical criticism approaches a biblical text as a "window" through which the interpreter seeks to view the past, literary criticism approaches a biblical text as a "mirror" in which are reflected universal human experiences. Thus, a literary critical reading is more immediately relevant to the experience of the interpreter than is an historical critical reading.

Formal/rhetorical criticism—For the past half-century or so, many biblical interpreters have adopted/adapted the principles of this twentieth-century school of literary analysis. The goal is to describe those literary qualities that make a text unique, that describe how it creates meaning. The emphasis is placed on the use of literary techniques (e.g., key words, themes, motifs, and structural patterns) and literary devices (e.g., metaphor, hyperbole, and irony). This type criticism describes how a text "works" to create the unique literary/symbolic universe of the text.

Narrative criticism—This form of literary analysis is based on the fact that, in addition to "real" authors and readers, many texts use the voice of "implied narrators/authors" speaking to "implied readers." Special attention is given to such features as characterization, protagonist and antagonist(s), setting, and plot in the construction of a "narrative world" wherein the text's meaning resides.

Structuralism—This methodology draws upon insights from cultural anthropology. The structuralist literary critic seeks to look beneath the "surface structures" studied in formal/rhetorical criticism in an attempt to analyze the "deep structures" of a text. Structuralists assume that all human activity, including the creation of literature, "reflects universal rules or codes, which they seek to decipher in order to understand the underlying meaning of the activity" being studied. "These codes are expressed in binary, polar opposites" such as love/hate, life/death, light/darkness, male/female, right/left, up/down, and good/evil. By deciphering the codes in a literary text, structuralists seek to uncover both the uni-

17

versal deep structures "hidden in the text and the text's particular symbolic universe."[11]

Having explored the importance of the metaphorical "glasses" every reader wears, and having explored many of the "tools" available in the biblical interpreter's "toolbox," we can now turn to a description of a process-informed approach to biblical interpretation.

---

11 Hauer and Young, 38.

CHAPTER FOUR

THE PROMISE OF A PROCESS HERMENEUTIC: KEY COMPONENTS OF A PROCESS APPROACH TO BIBLICAL INTERPRETATION

Occasionally, a new hermeneutical model will develop new exegetical methods (i.e., "tools"), but usually a new hermeneutical theory uses existing methodologies from a new perspective (i.e., a new tint in the "lenses" of the interpreter's "glasses"). The process hermeneutic has not developed any new exegetical methods; rather, its distinctiveness lies in its new perspective.

A process hermeneutic is a theory of interpretation derived from the process philosophy developed primarily by Alfred North Whitehead. Especially significant for the development of a process hermeneutic is Whitehead's understanding of perception and language.[12]

THE INDETERMINACY OF LANGUAGE

In Whitehead's philosophy one discerns a clear shift from Modernity's understanding of most language (i.e., as univocal, precise, and distinct; language as a literal description of reality) to Postmodernism's understanding of language (i.e., as analogical, imprecise, polyvalent, plurisignificant, and value laden). Philosopher and literary theorist Philip Wheelwright[13] distinguished these sharply divergent ways of understanding of language as *steno-language* (a symbol refers to one and only one thing) and *tensive language* (a symbol evokes a host of related things). According to

12 See especially Alfred North Whitehead, *Adventures of Ideas* (Macmillan, 1933; Free Press, 1967); *Process and Reality: An Essay in Cosmology* (Macmillan 1929; corrected ed. Free Press 1978); and *Symbolism: Its Meaning and Effect* (Macmillan, 1927; Fordham UP, 1985). For a detailed presentation of a process hermeneutic, see Farmer, *Beyond the Impasse*.

13 *The Burning Fountain: A Study in the Language of Symbolism, Metaphor and Reality* (Indiana UP, 1968); and *Metaphor and Reality* (Indiana UP, 1962).

Whitehead and Wheelwright, all language lies along a spectrum ranging from one hypothetical extreme—complete determinism (one-to-one)—to the other hypothetical extreme—complete indeterminism (one-to-everything). **(See Figure 1.)** Some forms of language strive to be closer to the hypothetical extreme of complete

Figure 1

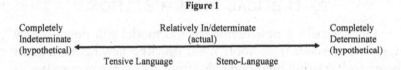

determinism (e.g., scientific language, rational argumentation, legal language, and everyday discourse), whereas other forms of language are located closer to the hypothetical extreme of complete indeterminism (e.g., poetry, metaphor, and religious language). Technically, all language is relatively indeterminant (or relatively determinant, if one prefers), but for biblical interpretation, the awareness that religious language is situated closer to the completely indeterminate end of the spectrum is of crucial importance.

The Evolutionary Nature of Texts

The imprecision of language affects both authorial expression and reader interpretation. Words cannot express exhaustively or precisely that which an author seeks to convey. Not only do words merely approximate a given proposition or idea, but they also evoke an indefinite number of related propositions. Thus, an author always "says" both more and less than she or he intends, and readers always "hear" more and less than the author intended. Even if the same proposition or idea is grasped by the author and readers, readers will "feel" it differently from the author—and differently from one another—due to the unique tint in the lenses of their glasses. **(See Figure 2.)**

Until recently with the rise of certain postmodern literary criticisms (like reader response criticism and process hermeneutics), most hermeneutical models assumed that the present meaning of

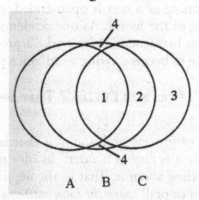

Figure 2

A   B   C

Circle A represents the propositions originally entertained by the author; circle B represents the propositions frequently elicited in the experience of the original readers; and circle C represents the propositions perceived by a later reader. Number 1 represents the propositions entertained by the author, original readers, and a later reader; thus, the possibility of genuine communication exists. Numbers 2, 3, and 4 represent the "growing edges" of text, i.e., propositions beyond those entertained by the author (due to the indeterminacy of language).

a text must be expressed in terms similar to what it meant when it was composed (i.e., authorial intent). For many interpreters, "what the text historically meant has become an essence from which its present meaning can only deviate within narrow confines." But if the text inevitably evokes new propositions over the course of time, "what the text might come to mean can theoretically be more important than anything the text has meant in the past." One could say that "potential meanings of the text remain encoded in its total capacity to elicit lures for feeling, until the kairotic[14] moment arrives." At the opportune moment, the givenness of a particular past, the contingencies of a particular present, and the possibilities for the future converge in the reading of a text, and a new meaning

14 The Greek word *kairos* refers to "opportune time" as opposed to "chronological, sequential" time (Greek *chronos*).

emerges.[15] Thus, according to a process hermeneutical model, the meaning of a text consists of the totality of propositions it can evoke. The meaning of a text is open-ended, evolving with the creative advance of the world. As one academic reviewer of my proposed process hermeneutic observed, "a process hermeneutic enables the Bible to become 'living word' once again."[16]

LANGUAGE AS "LURES FOR FEELING" THAT SPARK THE IMAGINATION

One tenet of process philosophy is that language does not so much *describe* a reality as it *lures*[17] us into particular ways of thinking and feeling about it. That is, the linguistic lures at work in a text (written or oral) *spark the imagination* about what is and, more importantly, what might be. Given this understanding of the function of language, the biblical text is more a source for *fresh proposals for imagining what is and what might be* than it is a *repository of static teachings*.

Because a text lures the reader, one of the goals of a close reading is to identify the lures at work in a text. This close reading requires "a bifocal approach to the text."[18] Some lures are readily identifiable; these more prominent lures are labeled *surface lures*. Other lures operate below the surface of the text at the presuppositional level; that is, they reflect the author's assumptions or presuppositions and so typically are implied rather than stated. Because they underlie the surface lures, they are termed *basal lures*. At times, basal lures may operate in a manner quite at odds with a straightforward reading of the surface lures. In such instances, one may speak of these basal lures as an *undercurrent*.

---

15 Barry A. Woodbridge, "An Assessment and Prospectus for a Process Hermeneutic," *Journal of the American Academy of Religion* 47:124.

16 Paraphrase of a comment made by an audience member at an academic conference in Kansas City, MO, April 9, 1989.

17 Although the word "lure" often has a negative connotation (e.g., to entice, tempt, or beguile into danger, difficulty, or evil), process thinkers use the word in its positive sense (e.g., to persuade, attract, influence, or evoke in contrast to negative terms like to coerce, force, and compel).

18 Russell Pregeant, *Christology Beyond Dogma: Matthew's Christ in Process Hermeneutic* (Fortress, 1978) 44.

Unlike most hermeneutical models, a process hermeneutic does not excise aspects of a text that are incompatible with the process worldview or that conflict with one another. On the contrary, a process hermeneutic encourages special attention to those dimensions of a text. What some hermeneutical models see as contradictions, a process hermeneutic attempts to view as *contrasts*. Careful consideration of lures foreign to the interpreter's own sensibilities, or lures that are at odds with other lures in the text, may result in the emergence of a novel pattern large enough to include both the foreign and the familiar in a harmonious contrast. A contrast is the unity had by the many diverse components in a complex phenomenon, for example, perceiving many colors in a unified pattern (as in a kaleidoscope) as opposed to perceiving only a single color. Contrast is the opposite of incompatibility, for an incompatibility is resolved by the exclusion of one or more elements to achieve a more trivial harmony. According to process philosophy, however, the more a subject can hold the items of its experience in contrasts, and contrasts of contrasts, the more it elicits depth and intensity of experience. When this occurs, the subject (in this case, the interpreter) experiences *creative transformation*. This is the ultimate hermeneutical goal—expanding one's horizon, becoming more inclusive, or simply put: spiritual growth.

In the final chapter I will illustrate the promise of a process hermeneutic by applying it to a notoriously problematic biblical passage, Revelation 4-5.

CHAPTER FIVE

AN APPLICATION OF A PROCESS HERMENEUTIC: REVELATION 4-5

BACKGROUND

Over a quarter-century ago at a meeting of the Society of Biblical Literature, John J. Collins offered a challenge to those of us interested in developing a process hermeneutic. He said that if we really wanted to convince biblical scholars that a process hermeneutic has promise, we should stop applying the hermeneutic to biblical texts that are "friendly" to process thought and instead apply it to something "challenging" something "antagonistic"— something like the Apocalypse to John. With this impromptu challenge, Collins unknowingly changed the focus of my biblical research for the next twenty years.

With the exception of fundamentalists, most Christians today voice grave reservations concerning the value of the Book of Revelation. Indeed, misgivings, suspicions, and outright rejection have plagued the Apocalypse throughout Christian history. Several early church leaders—for example, Gaius of Rome (ca. 210) and Dionysios of Alexandria (ca. 250)—regarded the book with suspicion. Martin Luther in/famously remarked: "My spirit cannot accommodate itself to this book. There is one sufficient reason for the small esteem in which I hold it—that Christ is neither taught in it nor recognized."[19] My colleague Tina Pippin wrote, "The Apocalypse is not a tale for women. The misogyny which underlies this narrative is extreme."[20] But in my opinion the most damning assessment of the book came at the hands of English novelist D. H. Laurence who observed that there appears to be two types of Christianity: "one

---

19 Quoted in Douglas Ezell, *Revelations on Revelation*: New Sounds from Old Symbols (Word Books, 1977) 15.

20 Tina Pippin, *Death and Desire: The Rhetoric of Gender in the Apocalypse of John* (Westminster John Knox Press, 1992) 105.

focused on Jesus and the command to love even our enemies, and the other focused on the Apocalypse and its portrayal of vengeance on and power over our enemies. Thus for Lawrence, Revelation is the 'Judas' of the New Testament because its portrayal of God's overcoming power—God as an absolute and brutally vengeful despot—betrays Jesus and his call to love."[21] Taking up John Collins' challenge, I decided to apply a process hermeneutic to what most interpreters would say is the least promising book of the Bible. For the purpose of this book I will limit my application to Revelation 4-5.[22]

EXEGETICAL ANALYSIS

Commentators frequently identify the notion of power as one of the deepest theological concerns of Revelation. The cosmic drama, set forth in what to modern readers is bizarre and confusing symbolism, can be characterized as a clash of powers. The Dragon (Satan), working through his henchman the Beast (the Roman government), wages war against the people of God.[23] The power the Beast exercises is clearly coercive, controlling, and unilateral. That God overcomes the Beast and the Dragon is also clear. The question to be answered in this exegesis—indeed, the most important theological and ethical question of the Apocalypse—is, "What is the nature of divine power? How does God conquer the Beast and the Dragon?"

The main title for God in the Apocalypse is *pantokrator*, a term variously translated "almighty," "all-powerful," "omnipotent," and

21 Farmer, *Revelation* 2. See D. H. Lawrence, *Apocalypse* (Penguin Books, 1974) 14-15. Interestingly, Whitehead himself called the Apocalypse "barbaric" in that its notion of "the absolute despot" leads to "the undoing of Christian intuition," by which Whitehead meant grace and love (*Adventures of Ideas*, 170).

22 Given the space limitation of this book, my exegesis will be suggestive not exhaustive. For a more detailed exegesis please see my *Beyond the Impasse*, chapter 8, and my commentary, *Revelation* from which the following comments are drawn.

23 Technically, the Dragon works through three henchmen: the Sea Beast (the Roman Empire), the Earth Beast (religion that promotes loyalty to the Empire), and the Great Whore (economic seduction that promotes loyalty to the Empire).

"ruler of all things."[24] Not surprisingly, then, almost all interpreters have simply assumed that the Apocalypse portrays, by means of its graphic mythopoetic language, the classical understanding of omnipotence that has dominated the philosophical and theological thinking of the Western world. Two aspects of classical theism's understanding of divine power are significant for the purpose of this exegesis. First, God is viewed as omnipotent in the sense of controlling or determining all that happens. Carried to its logical conclusion, this understanding of divine power denies genuine creaturely freedom and gives rise to the notoriously insoluble problem of evil. Second, classical theism understands divine power to be unilateral, flowing in one direction only: that is, power flows from God to all creatures but never the reverse. God affects all things, but nothing affects God. Consequently, the God of classical theism has been coldly but accurately described as "apathetic," incapable of feeling the feelings of others—impassive, unmoved, unchanging. To summarize, then, *classical theism understands divine power to be coercive, all-controlling, and unilateral in its operation.*

Certainly, one can list a number of biblical passages that appear to support classical theism's understanding of divine power. But a growing number of scholars, especially scholars informed by process theology, interpret some of the most profound biblical passages as pointing to a very different understanding of divine power.[25] The conception of power emerging from these passages contrasts sharply with that of classical theism. First, God's power is understood to be persuasive and all-influencing rather than coercive and all-controlling. God does influence every creature, seeking to lure or persuade or woo it toward the optimum mode for its development, but each creature remains genuinely free to choose the degree to which it follows the divine will. Second, God's power is

24 Nine of the 10 occurrences of *pantokrator* in the New Testament are found in Revelation.
25 For example, Genesis 1 pictures God as *wooing* creation out of chaos, not out of nothingness; Isaiah depicts the Servant of Yahweh functioning by means of a *gentle persuasion* that is willing to suffer, even to the point of death; the Gospels portray Jesus' opposition to violence in favor of *persuasive love*; Philippians 2 sets forth a *kenotic Christology* in contrast to a triumphalist Christology; and as this exegesis will demonstrate, the crucial Christological image in Revelation is *the Lamb who was slaughtered.*

portrayed as relational rather than unilateral, that is, power flows in all directions. Because reality is thoroughly interrelated, everything affects everything else. Not only does God influence every creature, but every creaturely event also affects God. God feels every earthly joy and sorrow. Thus, *God's power is understood to be persuasive, all-influencing, and relational.*

As the following exegesis reveals, one of the problems with most readings of Revelation is that interpreters have assumed that the book portrays classical theism's understanding of omnipotence. My conviction is that this mistaken assumption has prevented the majority of commentators from seeing the astonishing "revelation" disclosed to John. So, what does one see when the erroneous assumption is set aside? What does one see when one removes the distorting interpretive lens of classical theism's omnipotence?

Most interpreters assert that chapters 4-5 hold the hermeneutical key to unlock the meaning of the book as a whole. I agree. The way one interprets the key images of these two chapters, especially the symbolism of the Lamb, determines how one reads the rest of the book.

Chapter four opens with John being invited to enter the heavenly realm and see the things that must (a divine necessity) take place. Those familiar with the Hebrew prophetic tradition immediately perceive that John is being invited to observe the heavenly council where God's purpose is revealed. In keeping with the prophetic tradition, John is then expected to reveal to God's people the divine purpose and what part they are to play in implementing it.

Dominating chapter four—indeed, dominating the entire book—is the recurring symbol of the heavenly throne, a symbol of God's ruling power.[26] Unlike his probable source (Ezekiel 1:26-28), John refrains from an anthropomorphic description of the one occupying the throne (with the significant exception of 5:1, as we will see). Nevertheless, "the whole chapter is numinous with the divine presence."[27] The vision gloriously depicts God the Creator, the One who is worthy of worship. Indeed, God's holiness, power,

---

26 Forty-seven of the sixty-two New Testament occurrences of the word *thronos* are in Revelation, fourteen of which are in Revelation 4.

27 G. B. Caird, *A Commentary on the Revelation of St. John the Divine* in Harper's New Testament Commentaries (Harper & Row, 1966) 63.

eternity, and creative activity form the basis for John's assurance of the ultimate triumph of righteousness. What comfort this vision of the heavenly throne must have brought to those living under the oppressive shadow of Caesar's throne!

Chapter five opens with dramatic flair: a scroll lying on the open right palm of the One sitting on the throne. Although other interpretations have been proposed, most commentators are in general agreement with G. B. Caird: "the scroll is God's redemptive plan... by which he means to assert his sovereignty over a sinful world and so to achieve the purpose of creation."[28] The scroll has been sealed (perfect passive participle) with seven seals; hence, the scroll is securely sealed. Although the scroll rests in God's open hand, its opening awaits the emergence of a human agent[29] willing and worthy to break the seals, thereby revealing and implementing the content of the scroll. The announcement that no one in all creation—in heaven, on earth, or under the earth—was found worthy to open the scroll moves John to uncontrollable weeping. Will God's purpose for creation fail to be revealed and enacted for lack of a worthy agent?

John's utter despair sets in bold relief the proclamation by the elder that "the Lion of the Tribe of Judah, the Root of David" has conquered (aorist tense) so that he can open the scroll. That the elder's message is couched in traditional messianic imagery is noted by all commentators. Less frequently noted is the "martial ring"[30] of both expressions.

Now in reading Revelation, one is always wise to examine the dialectical relationship between what John hears and what he sees. Auditions and visions explain one another. An unfortunate paragraph break between verses 5 and 6 in most Greek editions and translations can cause the reader to miss the full impact of two contrasting images John has provocatively slammed together. John looks for the Lion of the audition but sees instead a Lamb.[31]

---

28 Caird, 72.

29 Other biblical examples of God's salvation being contingent upon a human agent include Rom 5:11-21 and Heb 2:5-18.

30 Caird, 73.

31 The most frequent symbol in the Apocalypse referring to Jesus the Christ is the Lamb; 29 of the 30 NT occurrences of *arnion* are found in Revelation.

The vision in verse 6 of a Lamb bearing the marks of sacrificial slaughter stands in stark contrast to the militant messianic Lion of verse 5's audition.

This is a most peculiar Lamb. The first peculiarity is that the Lamb is portrayed "*standing* as having been slain." In the vision the Lamb is very much alive! The perfect passive participle pictures the sacrifice as having been accomplished, with the marks of slaughter still visible. A second peculiarity is that the Lamb is described as having seven horns. Horns frequently symbolize power in Jewish literature, so the presence of seven horns indicates that the Lamb manifests perfect power. A third peculiarity is that the Lamb has seven eyes. Eyes frequently symbolize wisdom or knowledge; seven eyes indicate that the Lamb exhibits perfect wisdom.[32] By means of this jarring symbolism, "John asserted that *suffering, redemptive love is the most powerful force in the universe, an expression of the highest wisdom.*"[33] (The reader should note that what John expressed through the powerful imagery of mythopoetic language, Paul also expressed in the prosaic prose in 1 Corinthians 1:23-24, "Christ crucified . . . the power of God and the wisdom of God.")

Returning to the audition/vision dialectic, the audition (the militant Lion of Judah) explains the vision (the slaughtered Lamb): that is, the death of Jesus is not weakness and defeat but rather power and victory. Likewise, the vision explains the audition: God's power and victory (the militant Lion) lie not in brute force but in suffering, redemptive love (the slain Lamb). Now it is instruc-

---

Twenty-eight of those occurrences refer to the Christ; one (13:11) refers to the Earth Beast, a parody of the Christ. Note: Although a few commentators have argued that *arnion* should be translated "ram" because of "the wrath" (6:16-17) and victorious warfare of the *arnion* (17:14; cf. 19:11-21), the overwhelming philological evidence is that "lamb" is the proper translation.

32 Seven horns (power) corresponds to the Lion of Judah (Gen. 49:9-10); seven eyes (wisdom), to the Root of David (Isa 11:1-2).

33 Farmer, *Revelation* 64. As will become clear later in this exegesis, the expression "suffering, redemptive love" includes both the sacrifice of the Lamb and the faithful testimony to that act of love by the Lamb's followers.

tive to observe that this radical "rebirth of images"[34] (Lion/Lamb) contrasts sharply with the Apocalypse's portrayal of the nature of demonic power. In 13:11-12 John noted that the Earth Beast *looks* like a lamb but *speaks* like a dragon and exercises all the coercive power of the Sea Beast! (The reader should note that this is yet another interpretive vision/audition dialectic.) Clearly, the Earth Beast is a deliberate parody of the Lamb. By way of contrast to this Earth-Beast-in-lamb's-clothing, Christ's only power is that of the sword that issues from his mouth (1:16; 2:12, 16; 19:15), that is, words that pierce people's souls. "This imagery suggests that God conquers by means of a 'war of words'—persuasion not coercion, wooing not brute force. Thus, the paradox resulting from the dialectical relationship between what John hears (militant Lion) and what he sees (slaughtered Lamb) powerfully proclaims that *God's victory, God's conquest, is achieved only through redemptive love, a love willing to suffer if need be*."[35]

At this point I must pause to highlight a critically important distinction. Several modern commentators agree with my reading of Revelation 4-5 *thus far* (for example, G. B. Caird, J. P. M. Sweet, Eugene M. Boring, and David Barr). They agree that by means of the Lion/Lamb dialectic, John intended to redefine the nature of divine power. How their interpretations differ from what I propose in this exegesis can be illustrated by calling attention to Caird's summary statement, which is representative of the other commentators: "Omnipotence is not to be understood as the power of unlimited coercion, but as the power of infinite persuasion, the invincible power of self-negating, self-sacrificing love."[36] The first portion of Caird's statement clearly indicates that he viewed God's power as *persuasive* and *all-influencing* rather than *coercive* and *all-controlling*. However, the last part of his statement—"self-negat-

---

34 Eugene M. Boring ("The Theology of Revelation: 'The Lord Our God the Almighty Reigns,'" *Interpretation* 40 (1986): 266) commented: "as profound a 'rebirth of images' and redefinition of the meaning of 'power' as anything in the history of theology." David Barr ("The Apocalypse as a Symbolic Transformation of the World: A Literary Analysis," *Interpretation* 38 (1984): 41) observed: "a more complete reversal of value would be hard to imagine."

35 Farmer, *Revelation* 64.

36 Caird, 75.

ing, self-sacrificing love"—reflects classical theism's understanding of love, an understanding which is highly problematic. As liberation, African-American, feminist, and process theologians have argued, a "self-negating" or "no-self" theology—so characteristic of patriarchy and paternalism—is highly destructive to human personality, especially for the oppressed and marginalized. Instead of expressions such as self-negating or self-sacrificing, liberation, African-American, feminist, and process theologians use expressions like "redemptive suffering." This is more than just semantics. Redemptive suffering, you see, recognizes the *interconnectedness* of existence; consequently, redemptive suffering differs from both *self-centeredness* and its alter ego, *self-negation*, both of which deny the interconnectedness of existence. This is an utterly crucial recognition. Thus, what is missing from Caird's redefinition of divine power is the relational versus unilateral aspect. The relational aspect of divine power can, however, be discerned in chapter five and throughout Revelation, as the remainder of this exegesis will demonstrate.

In verse 7 the Lamb takes the sealed scroll from God's hand—causing the worship of chapter 4 to resume but shift its focus to the redemptive activity of God—and in 6:1 the Lamb begins to open the seals. Now in portraying that Jesus' sacrificial death enabled God to do what could not be done before—that is, open the scroll—John indicated that God's power is persuasive not coercive, all-influencing not all-controlling, relational not unilateral. The implementation of God's will is contingent upon the response of a willing and worthy human agent. At this point some interpreters might object that *this* particular human agent is the Christ, who is not merely human but also divine. Now I could enter into a discussion of a process understanding of Christology[37] to address this objection, but for sake of time, I will simply call attention to the fact that in the Apocalypse, John does not limit this *interdependent* relationship to God and the Christ. On the contrary, John proclaims his radical message of divine-human interrelatedness and interdependence in three bold ways.

---

37 For example, Ronald L. Farmer, "Jesus in Process Christology," in *Jesus Then and Now: Images of Jesus in History and Christology*, eds. Marvin Meyer and Charles Hughes (Trinity Press, 2001).

First, in verse 6b John observes that the horns and the eyes of the Lamb are "the seven spirits of God sent out into all the earth." The Spirit of God in all its fullness (i.e., *seven* spirits) is sent out as the horns and eyes of the Lamb. Apparently, John interpreted Isaiah 11 by Zechariah 3:8-4:10, where the seven lamps are "the eyes of the Lord which range through the whole earth," and the point is, "Not by might, nor by power, but by my Spirit." The earlier symbolism of the seven churches as seven lampstands (1:12, 20) would have prepared John's readers to understand the seven flaming spirits of God (1:4; 4:5) in terms of their own mission and witness.[38] Thus, John's readers were, or at least had the potential of being, Spirit-filled followers of the Lamb sent out to influence the world. By means of this symbolism, "John boldly asserted that *the continued activity of God in the world depends on the followers of the Lamb acting as the horns and eyes of the Lamb sent out into all the earth*."[39]

Second, throughout the Apocalypse John exhorts his readers to reject the counsel of the Nicolatians, the Balaamites, and Jezebel—counsel that amounts to embracing Roman society's definition of power. According to John, his opponents' understanding of power leads ultimately to evil and, thus, hinders God's purpose for creation. John counters his opponents' misconception of power by means of chapter five's radical rebirth of images and his recurring call for his readers to conquer *in the same fashion* as the Lamb conquered. The way of the Lamb, not the way of the Beast, will result in God's purpose for creation being accomplished.

Third, in the Apocalypse the scene continually shifts from earth to heaven and back again. As J. P. M. Sweet noted, in heaven are found "both the origin and the reflection of earthly events . . . [Indeed,] heaven's will waits on earth's response." Sweet further noted that in worship, "the heavenly will is communicated and becomes fruitful in earthly doing and suffering; [then] the earthly victory [or defeat] is registered . . . and becomes effective in new heavenly dispositions."[40] An excellent example of this interdepen-

---

38 A similar idea is expressed in narrative form in John 20:21-22.

39 Farmer, *Revelation* 64.

40 J. P. M. Sweet, *Revelation*, in *Westminster Pelican Commentaries* (Westminster Press, 1979) 113-14.

dent relationship of the earthly and heavenly spheres can be seen in the prayers of the saints on earth, which have their heavenly counterpart (e.g., the "golden bowls full of incense" in 5:8) and produce an effect on heavenly dispositions (e.g., "the censer . . . filled . . .with fire from the altar" in 8:3-5). But not only are good earthly deeds reflected in heaven, that is, deeds in which the divine will has been accomplished, but also reflected in heaven are earthly deeds resulting from the rejection of the divine will in varying degrees. Examples of evil being reflected in heaven include the sea before the heavenly throne (4:6), the souls of the martyrs under the altar who have been slaughtered because of their testimony (6:9-11), and the war in heaven (12:7-12). These evil deeds are also registered in heaven and affect new heavenly dispositions. Clearly the heavenly and earthly realms are thoroughly interrelated; what happens in one sphere deeply affects the other sphere.

Let us now summarize what this exegesis has revealed. "Jesus' sacrificial death may have enabled God to *inaugurate* the divine purpose, but the *continued* implementation of God's purpose depends on the followers of Jesus making his lifestyle their lifestyle." Throughout the book John appeals to his readers to conquer *in the same fashion* as Jesus conquered; that is, he calls them to be the horns and eyes of the Lamb sent out unto all the earth. "Obviously, heeding John's exhortation requires a radically new understanding of reality, one in which a slaughtered Lamb conquers and faithful testimony—accompanied by voluntary, redemptive suffering, even to the point of martyrdom if need be—results in the overthrow of evil and the establishment of God's purposes for creation."[41]

CONCLUDING HERMENEUTICAL REFLECTIONS

The preceding analysis has uncovered a cluster of *basal lures* by which John provided his readers a new perspective on power, both divine and human. The power that will triumph—that is, the power that will result in God's purpose for creation being achieved—is persuasive not coercive, influencing not controlling, relational not unilateral. But even if the preceding exegesis has convincingly demonstrated the existence of this radical *undercurrent* in

41 Farmer, *Revelation* 67.

Revelation, undoubtedly some interpreters will insist, and rightly so, that the *undercurrent* is not the whole picture. The dominant imagery of the Apocalypse as a whole (i.e., the *surface lures*) presents God's power as coercive, all-controlling, and unilateral. As was noted at the outset of the analysis, interpreters throughout the ages have felt that the major textual lures operate in this fashion.[42] Thus, my process-informed analysis has revealed a radical *undercurrent* working against the book's dominant surface imagery by means of *basal lures* suggesting that divine power be understood as persuasive, all-influencing, and relational. What is a reader to make of this paradox?

As was stated earlier, in contrast to most hermeneutical approaches, a process hermeneutic does not excise textual lures that are incompatible with the process worldview or that are at odds with other lures operating in a text. On the contrary, a process hermeneutic encourages special attention to these "problematic" dimensions of the text. The entertainment of lures foreign to the interpreter's sensibilities may result in the emergence of a novel pattern large enough to include both the foreign and the familiar in a harmonious contrast so that the reader's understanding of the text undergoes a creative transformation. How might this occur with respect to the discordant lures at hand: that God's power be viewed as coercive, controlling, and unilateral (the *surface lures*)

---

42 I acknowledge the problematic nature of the violent imagery of the central section of Revelation (chapters 6-20). In my commentary I wrote: "As the Lamb begins to open the sealed scroll, horrible violence and catastrophic destruction erupt. Indeed, the seven seals are but the first terrible wave in a long series that wash over the reader. . . . this violent imagery has led many interpreters to label the book un-Christian, the Judas of the New Testament. What are we to make of this disturbing feature? Is God, acting through the agency of the Lamb, the source of these horrors? If so, then John's portrait bears little resemblance to the Jesus of the gospels who rejected violence, forgave his persecutors, and taught his disciples to do the same" (Farmer, *Revelation* 70). But in addition to acknowledging the problematic nature of this disturbing imagery, I also offered a new way of reading the violent imagery, set forth in an excursus on pp. 70-74. The space constraints of this small book prevent me from presenting my suggestions here for how to read the violent imagery of chapters 6-20; for that, the reader is referred to my commentary.

and that God's power be viewed as persuasive, influencing, and relational (the *basal lures*)?

To begin with, the interpreter should note that it is a matter of conjecture as to John's level of awareness of the tension he created by means of this *undercurrent*. Being a product of the first century may have prevented him from perceiving what appears obvious—obvious at least in light of the preceding analysis—to modern interpreters operating with a radically different worldview. John may well have been unaware of the textual tension or paradox created by the following provocative lures:

1. His insistence on the necessity of a worthy human agent to reveal and implement God's purpose for creation.
2. His image of the slaughtered Lamb as the wisdom and power of God.
3. His call for the Lamb's followers to adopt the Lamb's lifestyle, rather than the lifestyle of the Beast, to insure the continuance of God's purpose in the world.
4. His portrayal of earthly events as not only reflected in heaven but also affecting heavenly dispositions.

As a first-century man, John would be expected to use the imperial and hierarchical terminology and imagery found in the surface lures; that was the shape of the world he inhabited. What is surprising is that his deepest assumptions about God created the undercurrent expressed in the preceding four lures—intentionally or unintentionally. But an author's basal assumptions always make themselves known in a text if an interpreter "listens" intently. That is why a process hermeneutic calls for a bifocal approach to all texts.

Whether John created this undercurrent intentionally or inadvertently, these basal lures nevertheless stand in tension with the deterministic worldview the surface lures imply. Moreover, whether John viewed the language of the surface lures literally or imaginatively is also a matter of conjecture. Even if John intended his language of the surface lures to be understood literally, present-day readers *may* view it imaginatively because all language, and especially mythopoetic language, is relatively indeterminate.

Furthermore, a process hermeneutic proposes that when the basal lures of a text function as an undercurrent to the surface lures, then the surface lures *should* be read imaginatively rather than literally. The reason for this hermeneutical proposal is that the basal lures form the deepest metaphysical assumptions undergirding the text as a whole and thus are the most important lures, even if the author did not *consciously* entertain these implied assumptions.

Therefore, when held in the unity of a contrast with the basal lures, John's deterministic language of the surface lures can evoke non-deterministic lures. The language of the surface lures evokes the firm *conviction* that God and God's people will eventually overcome evil. At the same time the language of the undercurrent evokes the *manner* of this overcoming of evil. Persuasive love that is willing to suffer if need be (the basal lure) will eventually triumph (the surface lure), because redemptive love (the basal lure) is the most powerful force in the universe (the surface lure). Thus, a process hermeneutic enables the Apocalypse to speak powerfully and relevantly to today's readers by issuing a transforming challenge to the modern world's understanding of the nature of power—both divine and human.

If a process hermeneutic can assist people today in perceiving the Revelation to John as *living Word*, imagine the promise this methodology holds when applied to less problematic biblical writings.

SUGGESTED READINGS ON PROCESS HERMENEUTICS

Beardslee, William A., John B. Cobb, Jr., David Lull, Russell Pregeant, Theodore J. Weeden, Sr., and Barry A. Woodbridge. *Biblical Preaching on the Death of Jesus.* Abingdon, 1989.

Cobb, John B., Jr., David J. Lull and Barry A. Woodbridge. "Introduction: Process Thought and New Testament Exegesis." *Journal of the American Academy of Religion* 47:21-30.

Cobb, John B., and David J. Lull. *Romans.* In the *Chalice Commentaries for Today* series. Chalice 2005.

Cobb, John B., Jr. "The Authority of the Bible." In *Hermeneutics and the Worldliness of Faith: A Festschrift in Memory of Carl Michalson. The Drew Gateway* 45:188-202.

_____. "Trajectories and Historic Routes." *Semeia* 24:89-98.

Farmer, Ronald L. *Beyond the Impasse: The Promise of a Process Hermeneutic* (Mercer UP, 1997).

_____. "Imagination and the Art of Interpretation: Reading Scripture and Tradition for the Sake of the World." In *Replanting Ourselves in Beauty: Toward an Ecological Civilization.* Ed. Jay McDaniel and Patricia Adams Farmer. Process Century Press, 2015.

_____. "Imagination and the Art of Interpretation: Seeking to Embody Schweitzer's Reverence for Life Ethic." In *Invest Your Humanity: Celebrating Marvin Meyer.* Ed. Julye Bidmead and Gail J. Sterns. Pickwick, 2015.

_____. *Revelation.* In the *Chalice Commentaries for Today* series. Chalice, 2005.

_____. "Undercurrents and Paradoxes: The Apocalypse to John in Process Hermeneutic." In *Reading the Book of Revelation: A Resource for Students.* Ed. David L. Barr. Society of Biblical Literature, 2003.

Ford, Lewis S. *The Lure of God: A Biblical Background for Process Theism.* Fortress, 1978.

Fretheim, Terrence E. "The Repentance of God: A Study of Jeremiah 18:7-10." *Hebrew Annual Review* 11:81-92.

_____. *The Suffering of God: An Old Testament Perspective*. Fortress, 1984.

Janzen, J. Gerald. *Job*. John Knox, 1985.

_____. "The Old Testament in 'Process' Perspective: proposal for a Way Forward in Biblical Theology." In *MAGNALIA DEI: The Mighty Acts of God. Essays on the Bible and Archaeology in Memory of G. Ernest Wright*. Ed. Frank Moore Cross, Werner E. Lemke, and Patrick D. Miller, Jr. Doubleday, 1976.

Lull, David J. "What Is 'Process Hermeneutics?'" *Process Studies* 13:189-201.

Lundeen, Lyman T. "The Authority of the Word in a Process Perspective." *Encounter* 36:281-300.

_____. *Risk and Rhetoric in Religion: Whitehead's Theory of Language and the Discourse of Faith*. Fortress, 1972.

Pregeant, Russell. *Christology Beyond Dogma: Matthew's Christ in Process Hermeneutic*. Fortress, 1978.

_____. *Matthew*. In the *Chalice Commentaries for Today* series. Chalice, 2004.

_____. "Matthew's 'Undercurrent' and Ogden's Christology. *Process Studies* 6:181-94.

_____. "The Matthean Undercurrent: Process Hermeneutic and the 'Parable of the Last Judgment.'" In Society of Biblical Literature 1975 Seminar Papers. Scholars Press, 1975

Suchocki, Marjorie Hewitt. "Deconstructing Deconstruction: Language, Process, and a Theology of Nature." *American Journal of Theology and Philosophy* 11:133-42.

Williamson, Clark M. and Ronald J. Allen. *A Credible and Timely Word: Process Theology and Preaching*. Chalice, 1991.

Woodbridge, Barry A. "An Assessment and Prospectus for a Process Hermeneutic." *Journal of the American Academy of Religion* 47:121-28.

_____. "Process Hermeneutic: An Approach to Biblical Texts." *In Society of Biblical Literature 1977 Seminar Papers.* Scholars Press, 1977.

_____. "The Role of Text and Emergent Possibilities in the Interpretation of Christian Tradition: A Process Hermeneutic in Response to the German Hermeneutical Discussion." Ph.D. dissertation. Claremont Graduate School, 1976.

MORE PROCESS THEOLOGY FROM ENERGION

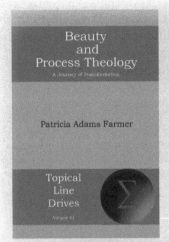

https://energiondirect.com/product/beauty-and-process-theology

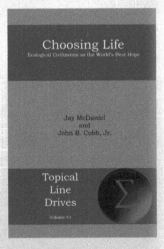

https://energiondirect.com/product/choosing-life

Both $5.99 paperback; $2.99 ebook